STEP-BY-STEP

Picnics

Picnics

ROSEMARY WADEY

SHOOTING STAR PRESS

This edition printed in 1995 for:
Shooting Star Press Inc
230 Fifth Avenue – Suite 1212
New York, NY 10001

Shooting Star Press books are available at special discounts for bulk purchases for sales promotions, premiums, fund-raising, or educational use. Special edition or book excerpts can also be created to specification. For details contact: Special Sales Director, Shooting Star Press Inc., 230 Fifth Avenue, Suite 1212, New York, NY 10001

ISBN 1-57335-006-0

Produced by Haldane Mason, London

Printed in Italy

Acknowledgements:
Art Direction: Ron Samuels
Editor: Joanna Swinnerton
Series Design: Pedro & Frances Prá-Lopez/Kingfisher Design
Page Design: Somewhere Creative
Photography: Joff Lee
Stylist: John Lee Studios
Home Economist: Rosemary Wadey

Photographs on pages 6, 20, 34, 48 and 62 reproduced by permission of
ZEFA Picture Library (UK) Ltd

Note:
Unless otherwise stated, milk is assumed to be full-fat, eggs are AA large and pepper is freshly ground black pepper.

Contents

✤

CHAPTER ONE

Elegant Picnics

An elegant picnic is suitable for many events, and lends a little grandeur to a special occasion. You could serve an open-air buffet at a garden party to celebrate a birthday or wedding; take one to a day at the races or an afternoon at the local regatta; or picnic during the interval at an open-air theater on a warm summer evening – the possibilities are endless.

The essence of this type of picnic is that it should be lavish. The venue should be perfect, the weather beautiful, and, most of all, the food should be splendid. Everything that is needed to make it so is packed up and taken along too. A table with a pretty cloth and proper china, cutlery and glass – no plastic or paperware for this picnic. The food should be similar to that served at an elegant dinner party, but take care to choose dishes that will still look and taste good when they have been packed up and transported some distance before being set out and eaten – and remember that you will not have all the usual advantages of final preparations in your own kitchen!

All this can be done with a little extra thought beforehand, very special packing, a careful driver, and then a beautiful setting for you and your friends. Don't worry about the washing up – simply pack everything away, and leave that for the next day.

Opposite: *Even if you don't have such elegant accessories as a fully fitted picnic basket, little finishing touches like fresh flowers and a champagne bucket can turn even a simple picnic into a special occasion.*

STEP 1

STEP 2

STEP 4

STEP 5

STUFFED EGGPLANT ROLLS

Long slices of eggplant are blanched and stuffed with a rice and nut mixture, and baked in a piquant tomato and wine sauce to serve cold as an appetizer.

SERVES 8

3 eggplants (total weight about 1½ pounds)
⅓ cup mixed long-grain and wild rice
4 scallions, trimmed and sliced thinly
3 tbsp chopped cashew nuts or toasted chopped hazelnuts
2 tbsp capers
1 garlic clove, crushed
2 tbsp grated Parmesan cheese
1 egg, beaten
1 tbsp olive oil
1 tbsp balsamic vinegar
2 tbsp tomato paste
⅔ cup water
⅔ cup white wine
salt and pepper
cilantro sprigs to garnish

1 Cut off the stem end of each eggplant, then cut off and discard a strip of skin from opposite sides of each eggplant. Cut each eggplant lengthwise into thin slices to give a total of 16 slices.

2 Blanch the eggplant slices in boiling water for 5 minutes, then drain on paper towels.

3 Cook the rice in boiling salted water for about 12 minutes, or until just tender. Drain and place in a bowl. Add the scallions, nuts, capers, garlic, cheese, egg, salt and pepper, and mix well.

4 Spread a thin layer of rice mixture over each slice of eggplant and roll up carefully, securing with a wooden toothpick. Place the rolls in a greased ovenproof dish, and brush each one with the olive oil.

5 Combine the vinegar, tomato paste and water, and pour over the eggplant rolls. Cook in a preheated oven at 350°F for about 40 minutes until tender and most of the liquid has been absorbed. Transfer the rolls to a serving dish.

6 Add the wine to the pan juices, and heat slowly until the sediment loosens, then simmer slowly for 2–3 minutes. Adjust the seasoning, and strain over the eggplant rolls. Set aside until cold, and then chill thoroughly. Garnish with sprigs of cilantro and cover with plastic wrap and foil to transport.

STEP 1

STEP 2

STEP 4

STEP 5

THREE FILLET PACKAGE

Fillets of lamb, pork, and chicken are layered with sage leaves, wrapped in spinach leaves and a layer of cottage cheese, and enclosed in puff pastry to bake and serve cold cut into slices.

SERVES 8

10–12 ounces pork tenderloin
about 12 fresh sage leaves
8–10 ounces lamb neck fillet
2 boneless chicken breast fillets (total weight about 10 ounces)
2 tbsp oil
3 cups large spinach leaves
12 ounces prepared puff pastry, thawed if frozen
1 cup plain cottage cheese
pinch of ground allspice
pinch of garlic powder
beaten egg or milk to glaze
salt and pepper

TO GARNISH:
sage leaves
cucumber slices

1 Layer the meat: cover the pork tenderloin with half the sage leaves, then add the lamb fillet, more sage leaves, and finally the chicken fillets. Secure with fine string and/or skewers.

2 Heat the oil in a skillet, and fry the layered fillets for about 15 minutes, turning regularly until browned and partly cooked. Remove from the skillet, and set aside until cold.

3 Blanch the spinach leaves in boiling water for 2 minutes, and drain thoroughly.

4 Roll out the puff pastry dough thinly into a rectangle large enough to enclose the layered fillets, and allow for 5 narrow strips to be cut off the edge. Lay the spinach down the center of the pastry dough. Spread with the cottage cheese, and season well with salt, pepper, allspice, and garlic powder.

5 Remove the string or skewers from the fillets, and lay on the cheese and spinach. Wrap up in the pastry dough, dampening the edges to secure. Place on a greased cookie sheet, and glaze with beaten egg or milk. Lay the strips of pastry over the roll, and glaze again.

6 Bake in a preheated oven at 400°F for 30 minutes until beginning to brown. Reduce the temperature to 350°F, and bake for an additional 20 minutes. Remove from the oven, and let cool; then chill thoroughly. Serve in slices garnished with sage leaves and slices of cucumber.

STEP 3

STEP 4

STEP 5

STEP 6

SEAFOOD PASTA

This attractive seafood salad platter is full of different flavors, textures, and colors.

SERVES 6–8

1½ cups dried pasta shapes
1 tbsp oil
4 tbsp French dressing (see page 77)
2 garlic cloves, crushed
6 tbsp white wine
2 cups baby button mushrooms, trimmed
3 carrots
2½ cups fresh mussels in shells
4–6 ounces frozen squid or octopus rings, thawed
1 cup peeled tiger shrimp, thawed if frozen
6 sun-dried tomatoes, drained and sliced
3 tbsp chives, cut into 1-in. pieces
salt and pepper

TO GARNISH:
24 snow peas, trimmed
12 baby corn
12 prawns in shells

1 Cook the pasta in boiling salted water with the oil added until just tender – about 12 minutes. Drain.

2 Combine the dressing, the garlic and 2 tablespoons of wine. Mix in the mushrooms and let marinate for at least 30 minutes.

3 Slice the carrots about ½ in. thick. Using a cocktail canapé cutter, cut each slice into shapes. Blanch for 3–4 minutes. Drain and add to the mushrooms.

4 Scrub the mussels, discarding any that are open or do not close when sharply tapped. Put into a saucepan with ⅔ cup water and the remaining wine. Bring to a boil. Cover the pan and simmer for 3–4 minutes until they open. Drain, discarding any that are still closed. Reserve 12 mussels for garnish, leaving them on the half shell; remove the others from the shells, and add to the mushroom mixture with the squid or octopus rings and shrimp.

5 Add the sun-dried tomatoes to the salad with the pasta and chives. Toss well and transfer to a large platter.

6 Blanch the snow peas for 1 minute and baby corn for 3 minutes, rinse under cold water and drain. Arrange around the edge of the salad, alternating with the mussels on shells and the whole shrimp. Cover with plastic wrap and chill until ready to transport.

PROVENCAL TOMATO & BASIL SALAD

These extra-large tomatoes make an excellent salad, especially when sliced and layered with fresh basil, garlic, kiwi fruit and onion rings, together with dressed baby new potatoes.

STEP 2

STEP 3

SERVES 6–8

1 pound tiny new or salad potatoes, scrubbed
4–5 extra-large tomatoes
2 kiwi fruit
1 onion, very thinly sliced
2 tbsp roughly chopped fresh basil leaves
fresh basil leaves to garnish

DRESSING:
4 tbsp virgin olive oil
2 tbsp balsamic vinegar
1 garlic clove, crushed
2 tbsp mayonnaise or sour cream
salt and pepper

1 Cook the potatoes in their skins in boiling, salted water until just tender – about 10–15 minutes. Then drain thoroughly.

2 To make the dressing, whisk together the oil, vinegar, garlic and seasoning until completely emulsified. Transfer half of the dressing to another bowl, and whisk in the mayonnaise or sour cream.

3 Add the creamy dressing to the warm potatoes, and toss thoroughly. Set aside until cold.

4 Wipe the tomatoes, and slice thinly. Peel the kiwi fruit and cut into thin slices. Layer the tomatoes with the kiwi fruit, slices of onion and chopped basil in a fairly shallow dish, leaving a space in the center for the potatoes.

5 Spoon the potatoes in their dressing into the center of the tomato salad.

6 Drizzle a little of the plain dressing over the tomatoes, or serve separately in a bowl or jug. Garnish the salad with fresh basil leaves. Cover the dish with plastic wrap and chill until ready to transport.

STEP 4

TOMATOES

Regular tomatoes can be used for this salad, but make sure they are firm and bright red. You will need 8–10 tomatoes.

STEP 5

15

STEP 3

STEP 4

STEP 4

STEP 5

DOUBLE CHOCOLATE TERRINE

The blend of white and dark chocolate mousse laced with rum, set in a loaf pan for easy transportation and serving, is finished with a fresh raspberry coulis and fresh raspberries.

SERVES 6–8

WHITE MOUSSE:
8 squares white chocolate
1½ tsp powdered gelatin plus 2 tbsp water
2 tbsp superfine sugar
2 egg yolks
⅔ cup sour cream
⅔ cup heavy cream, whipped until thick

DARK MOUSSE:
6 squares dark chocolate
2 tbsp black coffee (not too strong)
2 tsp powdered gelatin plus 1 tbsp water
2 tbsp rum
¼ cup softened butter
2 egg yolks
1¼ cups heavy cream, whipped

RASPBERRY COULIS:
1 cup fresh or frozen raspberries
about 1 tbsp confectioners' sugar

TO DECORATE:
fresh raspberries
whipped cream

1 Line a 9 × 5-in. loaf pan with plastic wrap, leaving plenty of overhang.

2 To make the white mousse, break up the chocolate, and melt in a bowl, either in a microwave oven on Medium Power for 2 minutes, or over a pan of gently simmering water. Remove from the heat, and stir until smooth.

3 Dissolve the gelatin in the water in a bowl over simmering water. Let cool slightly, then beat into the chocolate with the sugar and egg yolks, followed by the sour cream. Fold in the heavy cream. Pour into the pan and chill until set.

4 To make the dark mousse, melt the chocolate with the coffee, and dissolve the gelatin in the rum with the water, as above. Stir the dissolved gelatin into the melted chocolate, followed by the butter. Stir until dissolved then beat in the egg yolks. Fold the cream through the mousse. Pour over the white mousse and chill until set.

5 For the coulis, strain the raspberries and sweeten to taste with the sugar. Turn the terrine out, peel off the plastic wrap and decorate the top with the raspberries and whipped cream. Spoon the coulis around the base to serve.

STEP 1

STEP 2

STEP 5

STEP 6

ORCHARD FRUITS IN CARAMEL

An elegant fruit salad of poached pears and apples, oranges and strawberries in a wine and caramel syrup, topped with crumbled caramel.

SERVES 6–8

4 oranges
³/₄ cup granulated sugar
4 tbsp water
²/₃ cup white wine
4 firm pears
4 eating apples
³/₄ cup strawberries

1 Pare the rind thinly from 1 orange, and cut into narrow strips. Cook in the minimum of boiling water for 3–4 minutes until tender. Drain and reserve the liquor. Squeeze the juice from this and 1 other orange.

2 Lay a sheet of nonstick baking parchment on a baking sheet or board. Heat the sugar slowly in a pan until it melts, then continue without stirring until it turns a pale golden brown. Pour half the caramel quickly on to the parchment, and let set.

3 Add the water and squeezed orange juice immediately to the caramel left in the pan with ²/₃ cup orange rind liquor. Heat until it melts; then add the wine, and remove from the heat.

4 Peel, core and slice the pears and apples thickly (you can leave the apple skins on, if you prefer), and add to the caramel syrup. Bring gently to a boil, and simmer for 3–4 minutes until just beginning to soften – they should still be firm in the center. Transfer the fruits to a serving bowl.

5 Cut away the peel and pith from the remaining oranges, and either ease out the segments or cut into slices, discarding any seeds. Add to the other fruits. Hull the strawberries, and halve, quarter, or slice thickly, depending on the size. Add to the other fruits.

6 Add the orange strands to the syrup, and bring back to a boil for 1 minute, then pour over the fruits. Set aside until cold; then break up the caramel, and sprinkle over the fruit. Cover with plastic wrap and foil, and chill until ready to transport.

CARAMEL

The caramel will begin to melt when added to the fruit, so do this as near to serving as possible.

CHAPTER TWO

Winter Picnic Hamper

During the winter months there are often some lovely bright and sunny days. They may be chilly, but for those who like the outdoors, these are times to take advantage of. Everyone always gets hungry in the open air, so a picnic is just the answer for a day out in the country.

Begin the picnic with piping hot soup from a thermos, so you will quickly warm up. For a special day out, take mulled wine in a thermos to start the meal. Provide food which is substantial but not too filling, and pack it in containers from which it can be served, with just the lid needing to be removed. That will both protect the food from the elements, and cut the amount of space needed to pack it. Take good pottery mugs for the soup (and for coffee later), and either chunky china or good solid plastic-type plates. Remember to take a cake or cookies too, for everyone will get hungry later on, and these will go down well with a cup of coffee.

A blanket is a must, in fact several would be even better, for one can be used to sit on, and another used to wrap yourselves in if it is really cold! Food can be served from the hamper in the trunk of the car with very little preparation; there is no need to set up and lay a table, although a small portable table is always useful if space permits to stop things toppling over on uneven ground.

Opposite: A cold, bright day in winter is just as suitable for a picnic as a warm summer afternoon. Choose a sheltered spot in which to set up your picnic, and enjoy the fresh winter air.

CRAB BISQUE

This delicious creamy puréed soup, which is known as a bisque when made with shellfish or fish, is given a touch of brandy to warm up a cold day. Serve with rolls, such as the Cheese, Herb & Onion Rolls on page 24.

STEP 1

SERVES 4–6

1 fresh crab (about 1 pound) or 1 cup frozen
    crab meat, thawed
1 onion, chopped
2 carrots, chopped
2 celery sticks, sliced thinly
1 bouquet garni
6¼ cups water
3 tbsp butter or margarine
⅓ cup flour
1 tbsp lemon or lime juice
⅔ cup dry white wine
¼ tsp ground allspice
2 tbsp long-grain rice
3–4 tbsp brandy
6 tbsp heavy cream or natural fromage
    frais
chopped fresh parsley
salt and pepper

1 Remove the brown and white crab meat carefully from the cleaned shell, smashing the claws to remove the meat from them; then chop the meat finely. Chill until required.

2 Break up the shell, and put into a saucepan with the onion, carrots, celery, bouquet garni, and water. Bring to a boil. Cover the pan, and simmer for about 45 minutes. Strain the liquid, and reserve 4 cups. If using frozen crab meat, use fish bouillon cubes.

STEP 2

3 Melt the fat in a pan. Stir in the flour, and cook for 1–2 minutes without browning. Add the crab stock gradually, and bring to a boil. Add the lemon or lime juice, wine, allspice, and rice, and simmer for 10 minutes, stirring occasionally.

4 Add the crab meat, and simmer for an additional 10–15 minutes, or until the rice is tender, stirring from time to time.

STEP 4

5 Add the brandy. Reheat and adjust the seasoning. Finally, stir in the cream or fromage frais and 1–2 tablespoons chopped parsley. Reheat and pour into a warmed thermos for transporting.

6 Serve the soup in mugs, sprinkled with more parsley.

VARIATION

Smoked haddock can be used in place of crab; use the bones to make the stock.

STEP 5

STEP 4

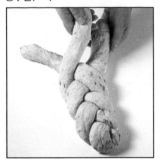

STEP 5

STEP 6

STEP 6

CHEESE, HERB & ONION ROLLS

A good texture and flavor are achieved by mixing white and granary flours together with chopped onion, grated cheese and fresh herbs, such as tarragon, thyme or sage, to make these rolls.

MAKES 10–12

2 cups white bread flour
1½ tsp salt
1 tsp dried mustard powder
good pinch of pepper
2 cups granary or malted wheat flour
2 tbsp chopped fresh mixed herbs
2 tbsp finely chopped scallions
1–1½ cups finely grated sharp Cheddar
   cheese
½ cake compressed yeast; or 1½ tsp dried
   yeast plus 1 tsp superfine sugar; or 1
   envelope easy-blend yeast plus 1 tbsp oil
1¼ cups warm water

1 Sift the white flour with the salt, mustard and pepper into a bowl. Mix in the granary flour, herbs, scallions and most of the cheese.

2 Blend the compressed yeast with the warm water, or, if using dried yeast, dissolve the sugar in the water, sprinkle the yeast on top, and leave in a warm place for about 10 minutes until frothy. Add the yeast liquid (or the easy-blend yeast and oil and water) to the dry ingredients, and mix to form a firm dough, adding more flour if necessary, to leave the sides of the bowl clean.

3 Knead until smooth and elastic – about 10 minutes by hand or 3–4 minutes in a food processor with a dough hook. Cover with an oiled plastic bag, and set aside in a warm place to rise for 1 hour, or until doubled in size.

4 Punch down and knead the dough until smooth. Divide into 10–12 pieces, and shape as you prefer – into round or long rolls, coils, knots or other shape of your choice.

5 Alternatively, make one large braided loaf. Divide the dough into 3 even pieces, and roll each into a long thin sausage. Beginning in the center, braid to the end, and secure. Turn the braid around, and complete the other half.

6 Place on greased baking sheets. Cover with an oiled sheet of plastic, and let rise until doubled in size. Remove the plastic, and sprinkle with the remaining cheese. Bake in a preheated oven at 400°F for 15–20 minutes for rolls, or about 30–40 minutes for the loaf.

RAISED TURKEY PIE

A filling of ground pork and bacon with diced turkey, pickled walnuts, mushrooms and herbs is enclosed in a hot-water pastry crust, to cut and serve in slices.

STEP 2

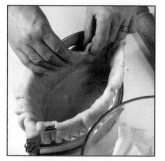

STEP 3

STEP 4

STEP 6

SERVES 6

FILLING:
12 ounces raw turkey fillets
1/2 cup ground lean raw pork
1/2 cup coarsely ground or finely chopped cooked ham
1 small onion, minced
2/3 cup button mushrooms, roughly chopped
1 tbsp chopped fresh parsley
good pinch of ground coriander
6 pickled walnuts, well drained
beaten egg or milk to glaze
1 tsp powdered gelatin
2/3 cup chicken stock
salt and pepper

PASTRY:
3 cups all-purpose flour
1 tsp salt
1/3 cup lard or white shortening
6 tbsp water
3 tbsp milk
beaten egg or milk, to glaze

1 To make the filling, chop all the turkey fillets and mix with the pork, ham, onion, mushrooms, parsley, coriander and seasoning.

2 To make the dough, sift the flour and salt into a bowl. Heat the fat in the water and milk until melted, then bring to a boil. Pour onto the flour, and mix to a smooth dough.

3 Roll out about three-quarters of the dough, and use to line a lightly greased raised pie mold or a loaf pan.

4 Put half the turkey mixture into the lined pan and arrange the walnuts over it. Cover with the rest of the turkey mixture. Roll out the reserved dough for a lid, dampen the edges and position. Trim and crimp the edge. Make a hole in the center for steam to escape. Garnish with pastry leaves, and glaze with beaten egg or milk.

5 Place on a baking sheet in a preheated oven at 400°F for 30 minutes. Reduce the temperature to 350°F. Glaze again, and bake for an additional hour. When browned, cover with a sheet of baking parchment.

6 Dissolve the gelatin in the stock, bringing just to a boil; season well. Let the pie cool for 10 minutes. Gradually pour in as much stock as possible through the hole in the lid. Set aside until cold, then chill thoroughly for at least 12 hours. Unmold to serve.

WALDORF SLAW

This salad combines the best of a Waldorf salad and a coleslaw in a tart yogurt dressing with an attractive garnish of carrot sticks.

STEP 1

SERVES 4–6

4 celery stalks, preferably green
$^1/_4$ white cabbage (about 8 ounces)
$^1/_3$ cup raisins
$^1/_2$ cup walnut pieces
4–6 scallions, trimmed and cut into thin
 slanting slices
2 green-skinned eating apples
2 tbsp lemon or lime juice
4 tbsp thick mayonnaise
2 tbsp natural yogurt or natural fromage
 frais
2 tbsp French dressing (see page 77)
salt and pepper
2 carrots, trimmed, to garnish

1 Cut the celery into narrow slanting slices. Remove the core from the cabbage, and shred finely either by hand or using the slicing blade of a food processor.

2 Put the celery, cabbage, raisins, walnut pieces and scallions into a bowl, and mix together.

3 Quarter and core the apples, and slice thinly, or cut into dice. Put into a bowl with the lemon or lime juice, and toss until completely coated. Drain and add to the other salad ingredients.

4 Whisk together the mayonnaise, yogurt or fromage frais and French dressing, and season well. Add to the salad, and toss to distribute evenly. Transfer to a serving bowl.

5 To make the garnish, cut the carrots into very narrow julienne strips about 2 in. in length, and arrange around the edge of the salad.

6 Cover with plastic wrap and chill until ready to transport. Alternatively, put the salad into a plastic food container with a secure lid.

STEP 3

STEP 4

VARIATION

This salad can be made using red cabbage for a change, and firm pears can be used instead of the apples.

STEP 5

STEP 2

STEP 3

STEP 4

STEP 6

MARBLED MOCHA CAKE

Chocolate- and coffee-flavored cake mixtures are baked together into a marbled effect which is topped with a rich coffee frosting.

SERVES 10–12

CAKE:
³/₄ cup butter or soft margarine
²/₃ cup light soft brown sugar
¹/₄ cup superfine sugar
3 eggs
1¹/₂ cups self-rising flour
2 tsp coffee extract
2 tbsp sifted cocoa powder
1 tbsp water

FROSTING:
¹/₃ cup butter
1¹/₃ cups sifted confectioners' sugar
1 egg yolk
1–1¹/₂ tbsp coffee extract

1 Grease and line a 7- or 8-in. round cake pan with nonstick baking parchment.

2 Beat the fat and sugars together until very light and fluffy, and pale in color. Beat in the eggs, one at a time, following each with a spoonful of the flour; then fold in the remaining flour.

3 Transfer half the mixture to another bowl, and beat the coffee extract into 1 portion and the cocoa powder and water into the other.

4 Spoon alternate spoonfuls of the 2 cake mixtures into the prepared pan. Swirl together lightly, and level the top. Bake in a preheated oven at 325°F, allowing about 1 hour for the larger cake pan or 50 minutes for the smaller one, or until the cake is well risen and firm to the touch. Let the cake cool briefly in the pan; then loosen and invert on a wire rack to cool completely.

5 To make the frosting, beat the butter until smooth, then beat in half the confectioners' sugar until smooth, followed by the egg yolk and 1 tablespoon of the coffee extract. Work in the remaining confectioners' sugar with sufficient coffee extract to give a piping consistency.

6 Using a large star tip, pipe an attractive design of shells over the top of the cake. Set aside to set. Place in a rigid plastic container to transport.

STEP 1

STEP 3

STEP 4

STEP 5

RUM & GINGER TRIFLE

Individual trifles of ladyfingers steeped in rum, candied ginger and ginger syrup with raspberries and orange rind, topped with custard and cream.

SERVES 6

about 24 ladyfingers
6–8 pieces candied ginger, chopped
grated rind and juice of 1 orange
2–3 tbsp candied ginger syrup (from the jar)
4–6 tbsp rum
1½ cups raspberries, fresh or frozen

CUSTARD:
scant 2 cups milk
3 egg yolks
1 egg
few drops of vanilla extract
2 tbsp superfine sugar
1 tsp cornstarch

TO DECORATE:
1¼ cups whipping cream, whipped
few pieces candied or crystallized ginger,
  chopped
gold dragées
strips of angelica

1 Break each ladyfinger into 3 or 4 pieces. Divide between 6 individual serving bowls, and sprinkle with the chopped ginger and grated orange rind.

2 Combine the orange juice, ginger syrup and rum, and spoon over the ladyfingers.

3 Arrange the raspberries over the ladyfingers, letting the fruit thaw, if frozen, when the juices will seep into the ladyfingers.

4 To make the custard, heat all but 2 tablespoons of the milk to just below boiling. Blend the remaining milk with the egg yolks, egg, vanilla extract, sugar, and cornstarch. Pour the hot milk onto the egg mixture, and return to a heatproof bowl. Place it over a saucepan of slowly simmering water, and cook slowly, stirring frequently until the custard thickens sufficiently to coat the back of a spoon. Do not let it boil, or it will curdle.

5 Cool the custard a little, then pour it over the fruit. Chill.

6 Pipe the cream over the custard with a large star tip. Decorate with the ginger, dragées and angelica.

32

CHAPTER THREE

At the Beach

A day at the beach brings a smile to the faces of children and adults alike, and to complete the day, nothing is better than a delicious picnic with lots of food to choose from.

The beach, of course, means sand, which can get into everything all too easily, so make sure the food is packed into containers with tight-fitting lids, and is wrapped in both plastic wrap and foil to give extra protection. Make the food suitable for eating with fingers or forks, so it can be taken straight from the containers, or transferred easily to paper or plastic plates.

Of course there are pebbled beaches and often grassy areas close by, where the sand won't be as much of a problem, as well as breakwaters and sand dunes – the main picnic can be set out in the most convenient place, which needn't be right by the water. As with all days spent outdoors, hunger pangs keep returning, and people like to pick and nibble throughout the day, and this should be kept in mind when deciding on the menu. Don't take just one portion of everything for each person; it is much better to take lots of smaller amounts of items such as Samosas or Spanish Omelet Squares, and a salad containing large pieces of raw vegetables, like crudités, is always a good standby.

Opposite: A picnic is the perfect meal to take to the beach, as all that fresh sea air makes people hungry, and even the simplest picnic will go down well.

STEP 2

STEP 3

STEP 4

STEP 6

SPANISH OMELET SQUARES

An oven-baked omelet with diced potatoes, onions, peas, tomatoes, herbs, and cheese is cut into small squares to make not much more than a mouthful.

MAKES ABOUT 36 SQUARES

2 tbsp olive oil
1 onion, thinly sliced
1 garlic clove, crushed
1 zucchini, trimmed and coarsely grated
1 red, green, or orange bell pepper, halved, cored, and deseeded
1 cup diced cooked potato
2/3 cup cooked peas
2 tomatoes, peeled, deseeded, and cut into strips
2 tsp chopped fresh mixed herbs or 1 tsp dried mixed herbs
6 eggs
1/3–1/2 cup grated Gruyère or fresh Parmesan cheese
salt and pepper

1 Heat the oil in a large skillet, and fry the onion and garlic very slowly until soft, but not colored, about 5 minutes. Add the zucchini, and fry for an additional 1–2 minutes. Transfer to a bowl.

2 Place the bell pepper on a broiler rack skin-side upward and cook under a preheated medium broiler until the skin is well charred. Let cool slightly; then peel off the blackened skin, and slice or chop the bell pepper flesh. Add the bell pepper to the onion mixture, together with the potato, peas, tomatoes, and herbs.

3 Beat the eggs together with 1–2 tablespoons water and plenty of seasoning; then add to the vegetables and mix well.

4 Line a shallow 8–9-in. square cake pan with nonstick baking parchment. Do not cut into the corners, just fold the parchment. Pour in the egg mixture, making sure the vegetables are fairly evenly distributed.

5 Cook in a preheated oven at 350°F for about 15 minutes, or until almost set.

6 Sprinkle with the cheese, and either return to the oven for 5–10 minutes, or place under a preheated medium broiler until evenly browned. Let cool. Remove from the pan and transport still wrapped in the baking parchment in an airtight plastic container, or cut into 1–1½-in. squares, and stack in a plastic container.

STEP 2

STEP 3

STEP 4

STEP 5

CHICKEN SATAY KEBABS

*Small kebabs of satay chicken with cubes of cheese and cherry tomatoes
added are served on crisp lettuce leaves.*

MAKES 8

8 wooden skewers, soaked in warm water
  for 30 minutes.
1 tbsp sherry
1 tbsp light soy sauce
1 tbsp sesame oil
finely grated rind of ¹/₂ lemon
1 tbsp lemon or lime juice
2 tsp sesame seeds
1 pound chicken breast meat, skinned
3 ounces Gouda or red cheese
16 cherry tomatoes
crisp lettuce leaves
salt and pepper

PEANUT DIP:
¹/₃ cup shredded coconut
²/₃ cup boiling water
¹/₂ cup crunchy peanut butter
good pinch of chili powder
1 tsp brown sugar
1 tbsp light soy sauce
2 scallions, trimmed and chopped

1 Combine the sherry, soy sauce,
sesame oil, lemon rind, lemon or
lime juice, sesame seeds, and seasoning
in a bowl.

2 Cut the chicken into 1-in. cubes.
Add to the marinade, and mix well.

Cover and set aside for 3–6 hours,
preferably in the refrigerator.

3 To make the dip, put the coconut
into a saucepan with the water,
and bring back to a boil; set aside until
cold. Add the peanut butter, chili
powder, sugar, and soy sauce, and bring
slowly to a boil. Simmer very slowly,
stirring all the time, for 2–3 minutes
until thickened; then cool. When cold,
stir in the scallions. Transfer to a small
bowl, and cover with plastic wrap and
then foil to transport.

4 Thread the chicken onto 8 wooden
skewers, keeping the chicken in the
center of each skewer. Cook under a
preheated medium broiler for about 5
minutes on each side until cooked
through. Set aside until cold.

5 Cut the cheese into 16 cubes, and
add one of these and a cherry
tomato to each end of the skewers.

6 Place each kebab on a crisp lettuce
leaf. Wrap in plastic wrap or foil, or
place in a plastic container. Serve with
the peanut dip.

STEP 1

STEP 2

STEP 3

STEP 4

SAMOSAS WITH SPICY DIP

A spicy filling of ground meat and vegetables enclosed in a pastry crescent to deep-fry and serve with a dip. They should be fried 2–3 hours before you leave for the picnic.

MAKES 16

FILLING:
1 onion, finely chopped
1 garlic clove, crushed
1 tsp freshly grated gingerroot
2 tbsp oil
1 carrot, grated coarsely
1¹/₂ tsp garam masala
¹/₂ cup cooked ground beef, pork or ham
³/₄ cup cooked peas
1 cup finely diced cooked potatoes
salt and pepper

PASTRY:
2 cups all-purpose flour
¹/₂ tsp salt
2 tbsp butter or margarine
scant ¹/₂ cup cold water
oil for deep-frying

CURRIED DIP:
²/₃ cup thick mayonnaise
3 tbsp sour cream or fromage frais
1¹/₂ tsp curry powder
¹/₂ tsp ground coriander
1 tsp tomato paste
2 tbsp mango chutney, chopped
1 tbsp chopped fresh parsley

1 To make the filling, fry the onion, garlic and gingerroot in the oil until soft. Add the carrot, and fry for 2–3 minutes. Stir in the garam masala and 4 tablespoons water. Season, and simmer slowly until the liquid is almost absorbed. Remove from the heat. Stir in the meat, peas and potatoes, and let cool.

2 To make the pastry, sift the flour and salt into a bowl, and rub in the butter. Add sufficient of the water to mix to a smooth, elastic dough, kneading continually. Cut the dough into 16 pieces, and keep covered. Dip each piece into a little oil or coat lightly with flour, and roll out to a 5-in. round.

3 Put 1–2 tablespoons of the filling onto one side of each round. Dampen the edge, fold over and seal. Cover the samosas with a damp cloth.

4 Heat the oil to 350–375°F, or until a cube of bread browns in about 30 seconds. Fry the samosas a few at a time for 3–4 minutes until golden-brown, turning once or twice. Drain on paper towels.

5 To make the dip, combine all the ingredients, and pack separately.

GARDEN SALAD

This chunky salad includes tiny new potatoes tossed in a minty dressing, and has a mustard dip for dunking.

STEP 1

SERVES 6–8

1 pound tiny new or salad potatoes
4 tbsp French dressing made with olive oil
   (see page 77)
2 tbsp chopped fresh mint
6 tbsp sour cream
3 tbsp thick mayonnaise
2 tsp balsamic vinegar
1½ tsp coarse-grain mustard
½ tsp creamed horseradish
good pinch of brown sugar
8 ounces broccoli flowerets
4 ounces sugar snap peas or snow peas,
   trimmed
2 large carrots
4 celery stalks
1 yellow or orange bell pepper, halved, cored
   and deseeded
1 bunch scallions, trimmed (optional)
1 head endive
salt and pepper

1 Cook the potatoes in boiling salted water until just tender – about 10 minutes. While they cook, combine the French dressing and mint. Drain the potatoes thoroughly, and add to the dressing while hot. Toss well, and set aside until cold, giving an occasional stir.

2 To make the dip, combine the sour cream, mayonnaise, vinegar, mustard, horseradish, sugar and seasoning. Put into a bowl, and cover with plastic wrap and then foil.

3 Cut the broccoli into bite-sized flowerets and blanch for 2 minutes in boiling water. Drain and toss immediately in cold water; when cold, drain thoroughly.

4 Blanch the sugar snap peas or snow peas in the same way but only for 1 minute. Drain, rinse in cold water and drain again.

5 Cut the carrots and celery into sticks about $2\frac{1}{2} \times \frac{1}{2}$ in., and slice the bell pepper or cut into cubes. Cut off some of the green part of the scallions, if using, and separate the endive leaves.

6 Arrange the vegetables attractively in a fairly shallow bowl with the potatoes piled up in the center. Cover with plastic wrap, and transport the dip separately.

STEP 2

STEP 5

STEP 6

STEP 1

STEP 2

STEP 3

STEP 4

ORANGE PECAN PIE

A really gooey and sticky pecan and orange pie, very tasty and just right for healthy appetites at the beach.

SERVES 6–8

DOUGH:
1¹⁄₂ cups all-purpose flour
pinch of salt
¹⁄₃ cup butter
1 tbsp finely chopped pecan nuts
4–5 tbsp iced water to mix

FILLING:
2 eggs
1 cup light soft brown sugar
generous ¹⁄₂ cup light corn syrup
grated rind of 1 large orange
1 tsp vanilla extract
1¹⁄₄ cups pecan nuts, halved
confectioners' sugar to decorate

1 To make the dough, sift the flour and salt into a bowl, then rub in the butter until the mixture resembles fine breadcrumbs. Stir in the pecan nuts evenly, then add sufficient of the iced water to mix to a firm but pliable dough. Knead lightly until smooth.

2 Roll out the dough and use to line an 8-in. fluted flan ring, pan or dish.

3 Arrange the pecan halves evenly over the bottom of the dough.

4 To make the filling, beat the eggs with the sugar, light corn syrup, orange rind, and vanilla extract. When evenly blended, pour or spoon over the pecans.

5 Place the flan ring, pan or dish on a cookie sheet, and bake in a preheated oven at 375°F for about 40 minutes, or until the pastry is crisp and the filling firm to the touch.

6 Let the pie cool completely, and then dredge lightly with sifted confectioners' sugar. Cover first with plastic wrap, then with foil for transporting. Serve the pie cut into wedges.

WALNUTS

This pie can also be made with walnut halves for a change. It may be frozen for up to 2 months.

WHITE CHOCOLATE BROWNIES

These moist chewy brownies, full of chopped nuts and raisins, are made with white chocolate for a change and topped with swirled mixed chocolate – just right to munch at the water's edge.

STEP 3

STEP 4

STEP 5

STEP 6

MAKES 8–12

2 squares white chocolate
¼ cup butter or margarine
1 cup light soft brown sugar
½ tsp vanilla extract
2 eggs
⅔ cup sifted self-rising flour
¼ cup finely chopped walnuts or other nuts
⅓ cup raisins

TOPPING:
2 squares dark chocolate, melted
1 square white chocolate, melted
confectioners' sugar for dredging

1 Line a shallow 8-in. square pan with nonstick baking parchment.

2 Break up the chocolate, and place in a heatproof bowl with the fat. Melt in a microwave oven on Medium Power for 2 minutes, or over a pan of slowly simmering water. Remove from the heat, and beat in the sugar and vanilla extract until smooth.

3 Beat in the eggs, one at a time, until smooth, then fold in the flour,

4 Add the nuts and raisins, and stir until evenly mixed.

5 Pour the mixture into the prepared pan, and bake in a preheated oven at 350°F for 35–45 minutes, or until the mixture is well risen, firm to the touch, and beginning to shrink away from the sides of the pan. Let cool in the pan; then remove carefully, and peel off the paper.

6 Melt the chocolates separately for the topping. First spread the dark chocolate over the top of the brownies. As it begins to set, trickle the white chocolate over it, and, using a fork or skewer, swirl the chocolates together to give a marbled effect. Let set. Dredge with confectioners' sugar.

7 Cut the brownies into squares, and transport in an airtight container, or wrap the whole pan in foil.

CHAPTER FOUR

In the Garden

A wrought-iron table or a wooden barbecue table makes an attractive setting for a garden picnic. A tablecloth looks nice with china and flatware rather than plastic or paperware, but don't use the best silver. If you keep the numbers small, it makes the occasion more friendly for everyone.

Choose a fairly simple but interesting menu, but not one that takes days to prepare, as you may spoil your own enjoyment if you give yourself too much to do. Often this is a good "spur of the moment" way to entertain friends, particularly when the day dawns fine and sunny or perhaps you have some house guests. Another idea is to take this picnic to someone else's garden, perhaps as a surprise party or just to save them from doing the cooking.

Opposite: The garden is an ideal place for a picnic, especially if you take a blanket and a picnic basket and do the whole thing in style – it doesn't matter if you are only a few feet from the house!

STEP 1

STEP 1

STEP 3

STEP 5

MELON WITH SMOKED SALMON MOUSSE

The refreshing flavor of the melon is offset beautifully by the rich salmon mousse and makes a most attractive and rather unusual appetizer.

SERVES 6

3 ripe small Charentais or Galia melons

SMOKED SALMON MOUSSE:
6 ounces smoked salmon pieces or slices
2–3 scallions, trimmed and sliced
1–2 garlic cloves, crushed
¾ cup light cream cheese
2–3 tsp lemon or lime juice
2–4 tbsp natural yogurt or natural fromage
  frais
salt and pepper

TO GARNISH:
pitted black olives
sprigs of fresh dill

1 Halve the melons and scoop out the seeds. For an attractive finish, scallop the edge by making short slanting cuts around the center of the melon using a small sharp knife, creating a zigzag design.

2 To make the mousse, put the salmon pieces into a food processor with the scallions and garlic, and work until smoothly chopped. Alternatively, chop the smoked salmon, scallions and garlic very finely, and mix together.

3 Add the cream cheese and process again until well blended, or beat into the chopped salmon mixture. Add lemon or lime juice to taste and sufficient yogurt or fromage frais to give a piping consistency. Season with salt and pepper.

4 Stand each melon half on a small plate, cutting a thin sliver off the base if it will not stand evenly.

5 Put the salmon mousse into a piping bag fitted with a large star tip and pipe a large whirl to fill the center of each melon, piling it up high.

6 Garnish each melon half with black olives and sprigs of fresh dill. When prepared, the melons may be chilled for up to 2 hours before serving.

VARIATION

Alternatively, halve a longer melon and cut into slices about 1 in. thick. Arrange 3 or 4 slices on the plate and pipe the mousse at one end.

STEP 1

STEP 4

STEP 5

STEP 6

CHICKEN WITH LEMON & TARRAGON

Chicken fillets are cooked with saffron, white wine, and stock flavored with lemon rind and tarragon, then the sauce is thickened with egg yolks and sour cream, and finished with mayonnaise.

SERVES 6

6 large boneless chicken breasts
$\frac{1}{4}$ tsp saffron strands
1 cup boiling water
1 tbsp olive oil
2 tbsp butter
1 garlic clove, crushed
$\frac{1}{2}$ cup dry white wine
grated rind of 1 small lemon
1 tbsp lemon juice
1–2 tbsp chopped fresh tarragon or 1 tsp
    dried tarragon
2 tsp cornstarch
1 egg yolk
6 tbsp sour cream or heavy cream
4 tbsp thick mayonnaise
salt and pepper

TO GARNISH:
fresh tarragon
lemon twists

1 Remove the skin from the chicken, and cut each breast almost horizontally into 3 thin slices. Season each piece well with salt and pepper.

2 Put the saffron strands into a bowl, and pour the boiling water over them. Set aside until they are needed.

3 Heat the oil, butter, and garlic in a skillet. When foaming, add the pieces of chicken, and fry for a few minutes on each side until well sealed but only lightly colored.

4 Add the saffron liquid, wine, lemon rind and juice, and half the fresh tarragon or all the dried tarragon. Bring to a boil, then simmer gently for about 5 minutes or until tender. Lift out the chicken pieces with a perforated spoon, and place on a serving dish in overlapping slices. Let cool. Boil the juices for 3–4 minutes to reduce slightly.

5 Blend the cornstarch, egg yolk, and cream together in a bowl. Whisk in a little of the cooking juices, and return to the pan. Heat slowly, stirring continuously until thickened and just barely simmering. Remove from the heat. Adjust the seasoning, and pour into a bowl. Cover and let cool.

6 Beat the mayonnaise and remaining fresh tarragon into the sauce, and spoon over the chicken. Cover and chill thoroughly. Garnish with sprigs of fresh tarragon and lemon twists.

ROSTI POTATO CAKE WITH ZUCCHINI & CARROTS

A mixture of coarsely grated potatoes, zucchini, and carrots with fried sliced onions cooked into a cake in a large skillet, topped with cheese and finished off under the broiler. Serve cold, cut into wedges.

STEP 1

SERVES 6

2 tbsp vegetable oil
1 large onion, sliced thinly
1 garlic clove, crushed (optional)
2 pounds potatoes
6 ounces zucchini, trimmed
4 ounces carrots
$\frac{1}{2}$ tsp ground coriander
$\frac{1}{2}$ cup grated sharp Gouda or Cheddar cheese
   (optional)
salt and pepper

1 Heat 1 tablespoon of the oil in a large skillet. Add the onion and garlic, and fry slowly until soft, but only barely colored – about 5 minutes.

2 Grate the potatoes coarsely into a bowl. Grate the zucchini and carrots, and stir into the potatoes with the coriander and seasoning until evenly mixed; then add the fried onions.

3 Heat the remaining oil in the skillet. Add the potato mixture and cook slowly, stirring occasionally, for about 5 minutes. Flatten down into a cake, and cook slowly until browned underneath and almost cooked through – about 6–8 minutes.

4 Sprinkle the top of the potato cake with the grated cheese, if using, and place under a preheated medium broiler for about 5 minutes, or until lightly browned and cooked through.

5 Loosen the potato cake with a large spatula and slip it carefully onto a plate. Set aside until cold; then cover with plastic wrap or foil, and chill until required. Serve cut into wedges.

STEP 2

STEP 3

ALTERNATIVES

This also makes a delicious vegetable accompaniment to any main course dish. Other vegetables can be used – parsnips, celeriac, leeks, and fennel, for example.

STEP 4

STEP 1

STEP 3

STEP 4

STEP 5

RUSTIC CHEESE BAR WITH CASHEW NUTS

Two kinds of flour, scallions, chopped cashew nuts, and cheese are baked into a bar to break off as required.

SERVES 8–10

1 1/2 cups self-rising flour
1 1/2 cups granary flour
1/2 tsp baking powder
pinch of salt
1/3 cup butter or margarine
1/2 cup cashew nut kernels, chopped
4 scallions, trimmed and thinly sliced
3 tbsp freshly grated Parmesan cheese
    or 3/4 cup grated sharp Cheddar cheese,
1 egg, beaten
about 1/2 cup milk
1 tsp lemon juice
1 tbsp sesame seeds

1 Sift the white flour into a bowl, and mix in the granary flour, baking powder, and salt. Rub in the fat until the mixture resembles fine breadcrumbs.

2 Stir in the nuts and scallions, followed by the cheese.

3 Add the egg and enough of the milk mixed with the lemon juice to mix to a soft but pliable dough. Transfer to a floured counter, and knead lightly until smooth.

4 Shape the dough into an oblong bar about 1 in. thick and 4 ins wide. Transfer to a well-floured cookie sheet.

5 Mark the bar into 8 or 10 slices with the back of a knife; then brush lightly with milk or water, and sprinkle liberally with the sesame seeds.

6 Bake in a preheated oven at 425°F for 20–25 minutes, or until well risen, golden brown, and firm to the touch. Transfer to a wire rack to cool. When cold, wrap in foil for transporting, or until ready to serve, broken or cut into slices.

FREEZING

The bar will keep well in the freezer for up to 2 months.

STEP 3

STEP 4

STEP 5

STEP 6

FRUITS OF THE FOREST CHEESECAKE MOUSSE

Red wine jelly with fruits of the forest set in a layer over a cheesecake mousse in a loaf pan to invert and serve cut into slices.

SERVES 6–8

1¹/₂ tsp powdered gelatin
4 tbsp water
2 tbsp superfine sugar
²/₃ cup red wine
1³/₄ cups frozen fruits of the forest
  (raspberries, blackberries, redcurrants,
  blackcurrants), just thawed

CHEESECAKE LAYER:
2 cups natural fromage frais
scant 1 cup light cream cheese
finely grated rind of 1 lemon
finely grated rind of ¹/₂ orange
1 egg
¹/₄ cup superfine sugar
1 tbsp lemon juice
1 tbsp powdered gelatin
3 tbsp water

TO DECORATE (OPTIONAL):
whipped cream
fresh raspberries and/or blackberries

1 Line a 9 × 5 in. loaf pan with a double layer of plastic wrap.

2 Dissolve the gelatin in the water, either in a microwave oven set on Medium Power for 40 seconds, or in a basin over a pan of gently simmering water. Let cool slightly; stir in the sugar, and then mix into the red wine.

3 Pour a thin (about ¹/₄ in.) layer of the wine jelly into the prepared pan and set aside until just set. Add the fruits and any juice to the remaining jelly, and spoon over the set layer, arranging the fruits attractively. Chill until set.

4 To make the cheesecake layer, beat the fromage frais, cream cheese, and fruit rinds together until smooth. Put the egg, sugar, and lemon juice into a heatproof bowl over a pan of simmering water. Cook slowly, stirring continuously until thickened sufficiently to coat the back of the spoon. Remove from the heat.

5 Dissolve the gelatin in the water and stir into the lemon mixture; then fold this through the cheese mixture. Pour over the set jelly, and chill, preferably overnight, until very firm.

6 To serve, invert carefully, and remove the plastic wrap. Decorate with whipped cream and raspberries if liked.

STEP 2

STEP 3

STEP 4

STEP 6

FLORENTINE TWISTS

These famous and delicious Florentine cookies are twisted into curls or cones as they are removed from the cookie sheets, and then just the ends are dipped in chocolate.

MAKES ABOUT 20

¹/₃ cup butter
¹/₂ cup superfine sugar
¹/₂ cup roughly chopped blanched or slivered almonds
3 tbsp chopped raisins
¹/₄ cup chopped mixed peel
scant ¹/₄ cup chopped candied cherries
3 tbsp finely chopped dried apricots
finely grated rind of ¹/₂ lemon or ¹/₂ small orange
about 4 squares dark or white chocolate

1 Line 2–3 cookie sheets with nonstick baking parchment; and grease 4–6 cornets (cream roll forms), or a fairly thin rolling pin, or wooden spoon handles.

2 Melt the butter and sugar together slowly in a saucepan, and then bring to a boil for 1 minute. Remove the pan from the heat, and stir in all the remaining ingredients, except the chocolate. Let cool.

3 Put heaped teaspoonfuls of the mixture onto the cookie sheets, keeping them well apart, only 3–4 per sheet, and flatten slightly.

4 Bake in a preheated oven at 350°F for 10–12 minutes, or until golden-brown. Let cool until they begin to firm up. As they cool, press the edges back to form a neat shape. Remove each one carefully with a spatula, and wrap quickly around a cornet, or lay over the rolling pin or spoon handles. If they become too firm to bend, return to the oven briefly to soften again.

5 Set aside until cold and crisp and then slip carefully off the cornets or remove from the rolling pin or spoons.

6 Melt the chocolate in a heatproof bowl over a saucepan of hot water, or in a microwave oven set on Full Power for about 45 seconds, and stir until smooth. Either dip the end of each Florentine twist into the chocolate, or, using a pastry brush, paint chocolate to come about halfway up the twist. As the chocolate sets, it can be marked into wavy lines with a fork. Set aside to set.

CHAPTER FIVE

A Teenage Picnic

Young people seem to be continually on the move, always doing something or going somewhere, and they are always hungry. They find their entertainment in many ways; it may be playing or watching sport, a cycle ride or trip to an amusement park, or more simply just "going out for the day – but please could we have some food!"

Forks, fingers, and paper plates are the order of the day with bottles or cans of fruit drinks or soda to accompany a menu that should have plenty of choice to cater for all fads and fancies, as well as healthy appetites. If any food containers as well as the paperware can be discarded after the picnic, so much the better (use large margarine and yogurt cartons with airtight lids, for example) – simply provide a couple of garbage bags for disposal of the garbage.

Such food as crudités, small nutburgers, and slices of pie are excellent, because they are easy to eat and filling as well as tasty. If salad is included, this can be put into individual bowls, and other items can be added at will. The general rule is that "bits and pieces" in small amounts go down best of all, and allow for continual replenishments to satisfy those healthy appetites.

Opposite: Some simple, filling food and a suitable setting are all you need for an impromptu picnic.

STEP 1

STEP 2

STEP 4

STEP 6

VERONICA SALAD

A delicious salad of strips of cooked chicken with grapes, celery, and hard-cooked eggs in a lightly curried, minty dressing garnished with endive and grapes.

SERVES 6

4 boneless chicken breasts, trimmed
2 tbsp olive oil
1 tbsp sunflower or vegetable oil
1–2 garlic cloves, crushed
1 onion, finely chopped
2 tbsp chopped fresh mint
4 green celery stalks
1 1/2 cups black grapes, preferably seedless
1 cup large green seedless grapes
2 tbsp butter or margarine
1 tbsp all-purpose flour
1/2 tsp curry powder
3 tbsp white wine or stock
5 tbsp milk
2 tbsp natural fromage frais
2 tbsp mayonnaise or salad cream
1 head endive
2 hard-cooked eggs
salt and pepper

1 Cut the chicken into narrow strips, removing any skin and gristle. Heat the oils in a skillet. Add the garlic and chicken, and fry slowly until well sealed. Add the onion, and continue to fry until both the chicken and onion are tender.

2 Stir in the mint and plenty of seasoning. Drain off the oil and any juices immediately, and put the chicken mixture into a bowl. Set aside until cold.

3 Cut the celery into narrow slanting slices. Add to the chicken.

4 Reserve a few whole black grapes for garnish. If they are large or contain seeds, cut the rest in half. Remove any seeds, and then add to the salad with the green grapes.

5 Melt the fat in a pan. Stir in the flour and curry powder, and cook for 1–2 minutes. Add the wine and milk, and bring to a boil, simmering until thick. Remove from the heat. Season well, and stir in the fromage frais. Cover with plastic wrap, and set aside until cold.

6 Add the mayonnaise or salad cream to the sauce, and add to the chicken mixture, tossing evenly. Turn into a serving dish. Cut the endive leaves into lengths of 2 inches and arrange around the edge of the salad with the reserved grapes and quarters of hard-cooked egg. Cover and chill until needed.

STEP 1

STEP 2

STEP 3

STEP 4

NUTBURGERS WITH CHEESE

A delicious mixture of chopped nuts, onion, garlic, herbs, carrot, and Parmesan cheese shaped into small balls, dipped in egg and crumbs to fry and serve cold.

MAKES 12

1 onion, finely chopped
1 garlic clove, crushed
1 tbsp olive oil
1/4 cup all-purpose flour
1/2 cup vegetable stock or milk
2 cups chopped mixed nuts (including
  cashews, hazelnuts, and walnuts)
1 cup fresh breadcrumbs
2 carrots, grated coarsely
1 tbsp chopped fresh parsley
1 tbsp dried thyme
2 tbsp grated Parmesan cheese
1 tbsp lemon juice
1 tsp vegetable extract
1 egg, beaten
dried bread crumbs
oil for deep-frying (optional)
mixed salad greens to serve
salt and pepper

1 Fry the onion and garlic slowly in the oil until soft. Stir in the flour, and cook for 1–2 minutes. Add the stock or milk gradually, and bring to a boil.

2 Remove from the heat, and stir in the nuts, bread crumbs, carrots, herbs, Parmesan cheese, lemon juice, vegetable extract, and seasoning. Set aside until cold.

3 Divide the mixture into 12, and roll into even-sized balls.

4 Dip each piece first in beaten egg, and then coat in breadcrumbs.

5 Place on a well-greased cookie sheet, and bake in a preheated oven at 350°F for about 20 minutes, or until lightly browned and crisp. Alternatively, deep-fry in oil heated to 350°F for 3–4 minutes until golden-brown. The oil is at the correct temperature for deep-frying when a cube of bread browns in it in 30 seconds.

6 Drain on crumpled paper towels, and, when cold, arrange on a platter on a mixture of salad greens. Cover with plastic wrap or foil to transport.

VARIATION

These nutburgers can be made into miniature bite-sized balls if preferred, and they make excellent cocktail snacks.

STEP 2

STEP 3

STEP 4

STEP 4

POACHER'S BRAID

An elegant puff or plain pastry braid filled with a mixture of sausage meat, bacon, onion, mushrooms, and sage to serve cut in slices, to eat with a fork or in your fingers.

SERVES 4–6

DOUGH:
2 cups all-purpose flour
pinch of salt
¼ cup lard or white shortening
¼ cup butter or block margarine
cold water to mix
beaten egg or top of the milk to glaze
OR 12 ounces prepared puff pastry

FILLING:
1 pound pork sausage meat
¾ cup chopped, rindless lean bacon
1 onion, chopped finely
1 garlic clove, crushed
1 cup chopped mushrooms
1 tsp chopped fresh sage or ½ tsp dried sage
salt and pepper

1 To make the dough, sift the flour and salt into a bowl, and rub in the fat until the mixture resembles fine breadcrumbs. Add sufficient water to mix to a pliable dough. Knead lightly; then wrap in foil, and chill.

2 To make the filling, combine the sausage meat, bacon, onion, garlic, mushrooms, sage, a little salt, and plenty of pepper until evenly mixed.

3 Roll out the dough on a lightly floured counter to a 12-in. square. Place the sausage meat mixture in a block evenly down the center, leaving a 1-in. margin at the top and base. Make cuts at 1-in. intervals down both sides of the pastry to within 1½ inches of the filling.

4 Fold the top and bottom ends up over the filling, and then cover the filling with alternate strips of pastry, first from one side and then the other, to make a braid.

5 Transfer the braid carefully to a lightly greased or dampened cookie sheet, and glaze thoroughly with beaten egg or milk.

6 Bake in a preheated oven at 425°F for 20 minutes; then reduce the temperature to 350°F and bake for an additional 30–40 minutes until golden-brown and crisp. Let cool; then wrap in foil, and chill until ready to transport. Serve cut into slices.

CRUDITES WITH DIPS

Crunchy fresh vegetables, tortilla chips, and snacks served with three very different dips are easy to dunk and munch. Transport the dips in small bowls covered with plastic wrap and foil.

STEP 1

SERVES 6

¹/₄ English cucumber
2–3 carrots
3 celery stalks
1 green bell pepper, halved, cored, and
 deseeded
¹/₂ small cauliflower or head broccoli
1 bunch radishes, trimmed
4-ounce package tortilla chips
about 30 breadsticks

CURRIED DIP:
2 hard-cooked eggs, finely grated or chopped
4 tbsp natural fromage frais
2 tbsp thick mayonnaise
1 garlic clove, crushed
1 tsp curry powder
good pinch of ground apple pie spice
salt and pepper

GARLIC CHEESE DIP:
scant 1 cup light cream cheese
2 garlic cloves, crushed
2–3 tsp lemon or lime juice
4 scallions, trimmed and chopped finely

SMOKED MACKEREL DIP:
1 tbsp very finely chopped onion
³/₄ cup smoked mackerel fillet, skinned and
 flaked
finely grated rind of ¹/₄–¹/₂ lemon

2 tsp lemon juice
4 tbsp natural fromage frais or sour cream
1 tbsp chopped fresh parsley

1 Cut the cucumber, carrots, and celery into sticks about 2 ins long. Cut the bell pepper into strips, and divide the cauliflower or broccoli into small flowerets. Put each vegetable separately into a small plastic bag for transportation.

2 To make the Curried Dip, combine all the ingredients, and season to taste.

3 To make the Garlic Cheese Dip, combine all the ingredients, and season to taste.

4 To make the Smoked Mackerel Dip, blend all the ingredients together until well mixed, and season to taste with salt and pepper.

5 To serve, place the bowls of dips in the center of a large platter and arrange the vegetables, tortilla chips, and breadsticks around the bowls.

STEP 2

STEP 3

STEP 4

STEP 1

STEP 3

STEP 4

STEP 5

BANANA PICNIC LOAF

Mashed bananas with dried apricots or prunes and nuts are made into a delicious cake to be cut into slices and eaten either plain or spread with butter.

MAKES 12 SLICES

1 cup light soft brown sugar
½ cup butter or margarine
2 eggs
2–3 peeled ripe bananas
grated rind of 1 lemon
2 tsp lemon juice
2 cups self-rising flour
½ tsp ground cinnamon
¼ tsp baking soda
½ cup chopped, no-need-to-soak dried
   apricots or prunes
½ cup roughly chopped walnut pieces
sifted confectioners' sugar for dredging

1 Grease and line a 9 × 5-in. loaf pan with nonstick baking parchment.

2 Beat the sugar and fat together until light and fluffy, and pale in color. Beat in the eggs, one at a time.

3 Mash the bananas with the lemon rind and juice, and beat into the cake mixture.

4 Sift the flour, cinnamon, and baking soda together, and fold evenly into the cake mixture, followed by the chopped apricots or prunes and walnuts.

5 Turn into the pan, and level the top. Bake in a preheated oven at 350°F for about 50 minutes, or until firm to the touch and a skewer inserted in the loaf comes out clean. Let cool in the pan for 10 minutes, then invert on a wire rack, and let cool completely.

6 Before transporting, remove the paper from around the cake; sprinkle the top with sifted confectioners' sugar, and wrap in foil to carry. Serve cut into slices or wedges.

FREEZING

This cake may be frozen for up to 3 months.

STEP 3

STEP 4

STEP 5

STEP 6

BELGIAN APRICOT TORTE

An unusual type of shortbread dough flavored with orange and lemon rind which is grated into the pan with a rich apricot mixture in the center. When cooked, it is dredged heavily with confectioners' sugar and cut into wedges to serve.

MAKES 8–10

$^3/_4$ cup butter
$^1/_4$ cup superfine sugar
$1^1/_2$ tbsp oil
$^1/_2$ tsp vanilla extract
1 egg, beaten
3 cups all-purpose flour
$1^1/_2$ tsp baking powder
grated rind of 1 lemon
grated rind of 1 orange
$^1/_2$ cup apricot jam
$^1/_2$ cup finely chopped no-need-to-soak dried
    apricots
confectioners' sugar for dredging

1 Line a 7–8-in. round cake pan with nonstick baking parchment.

2 Beat the butter until soft, then beat in the sugar, and continue until light and fluffy. Beat in the oil. Add the vanilla extract and egg, and beat well.

3 Sift the flour with the baking powder, and gradually work into the creamed mixture with the grated lemon and orange rinds. Knead together as for a shortbread dough. Divide the dough in half, and coarsely grate one portion of it into the pan so it covers the bottom evenly.

4 Beat the jam until smooth, then beat in the chopped apricots. Spread the apricot mixture evenly over the dough, taking it right to the edges.

5 Grate the remaining dough evenly over the jam, and cook in a preheated oven at 300°F for about $1–1^1/_4$ hours, or until lightly browned and just firm. Remove from the oven, and set aside until cold.

6 Remove the torte from the pan and strip off the paper. Dredge heavily with sifted confectioners' sugar. Either wrap in foil, or place in an airtight plastic container to transport.

FREEZING

This cake can successfully be frozen for up to 3 months. Add the confectioners' sugar when the cake has thawed. It will keep for at least a week in the refrigerator.

ORGANIZING A PICNIC

COOKED SALAD DRESSING

For those who like salad dressing rather than mayonnaise, this is an easy way to produce a delicious dressing. It will keep in an airtight container in the refrigerator for about 5 days.

$1\frac{1}{2}$ tbsp all-purpose flour
$1\frac{1}{2}$ tsp superfine sugar
1 tsp dried mustard powder
6 tbsp milk
2 tbsp butter
1 egg, beaten
3–4 tbsp wine or tarragon
   vinegar
4 tbsp sunflower or vegetable
   oil
salt and white pepper

1. Mix together the flour, sugar, mustard, and seasonings, and stir in the milk gradually until smoothly blended.
2. Bring slowly to a boil, stirring continuously, and simmer for 1 minute.
3. Remove from the heat, and let cool slightly, then beat in the butter until melted, followed by the egg. Return to a low heat, and cook to just below boiling point, stirring continuously. Do not let boil, or it may curdle.
4. Remove from the heat, and beat in the vinegar to taste gradually, followed by the oil. Adjust the seasonings. Cover and let cool. Transfer to an airtight container, and chill.

THE PERFECT PICNIC

A picnic can vary from a simple and impromptu affair to a well-organized and thoughtfully planned outing. The occasion can vary: you might take a picnic to a sporting event, such as a local football match or baseball game, to save having to find food when you get there, and to give an informal outing a sense of occasion. At the other end of the scale, you might organize a truly stylish, sophisticated, and elegant picnic, which includes a proper table set with china, silver, and glass, either as an event in its own right, held in your garden as an alternative to a dinner party, or to accompany a visit to the races, or perhaps to an open-air concert or theater. But whatever the occasion or style of the picnic, the pleasure of eating outdoors is always the same, and people's appetites and their appreciation of the food are always enhanced by the fresh air and the unusual setting for a meal.

The location

When you have time to plan your picnic, do try to pick a pretty place with a certain amount of shade, reasonably level ground (particularly if you are taking a portable table) and some shelter, especially if you are at the beach, as even a light breeze can blow sand into your food. Many people like to find a tree, hedge, or similar landmark, rather than use an open spot in the middle of a field, particularly if you need shelter from the sun or wind.

Packing for the picnic

With a little thought and care, most food can be packed so that it arrives at its destination fresh and appetizing. Throughout this book you will find advice on how best to transport the finished dishes. However, if there is a bumpy drive to the venue, extra care will be needed with the packing.

Large picnic hampers or rigid boxes are essential when elegant picnics are to be transported, and often the glass and china need even more careful packaging than the food itself! Beware of using newspaper, as the ink can rub off onto your best china and glass, and make everything look grubby. Use brown paper or tissue paper first, and then newspaper or bubblewrap to cushion it more. If you are taking dishcloths and napkins, they can be put to good use by being wrapped around precious items, or used to fill a gap in the packing.

Remember to pack all the other essentials as well as the food and basic dishes. There is nothing worse than going to a lot of trouble with the food, and then arriving to find you have forgotten the condiments, the bread knife, or, most important, the corkscrew! Finally, always take some spare plastic garbage bags, and clear up completely after your picnic. Take all your garbage home to dispose of safely and properly.

The impromptu picnic

Even if your picnic is a last-minute affair, brought about by an unexpected hot and sunny day when a trip to the shore or the riverside suddenly becomes an excellent idea, the food can still be imaginative and delicious. Choose food that can be quickly prepared, that is suitable to eat with the fingers or possibly a fork, and that can be casually packed in foil or plastic containers that can also act as serving dishes. Choose food that will pack easily, so that it arrives intact and still looking its best.

The only accessories necessary for an informal picnic are perhaps paper plates, a few paper napkins or some paper towels, plastic or paper cups or mugs for the ever-essential thermos of coffee, and a corkscrew if you are taking wine.

PLANNING THE MENU
If possible, a selection of food is best for a picnic, as appetites are always more healthy in "the great outdoors" and even the most modest of eaters seem to consume enormous amounts of food. Having a selection of food will also help you to avoid any food dislikes or allergies, and cater for all tastes, especially if some of the guests are unknown to you. You should in any case always cater for non-fish eaters, vegetarians and so on, and provide plenty of salads and simple food for those who prefer to eat lightly.

For impromptu picnics, sandwiches are excellent, as they can be assembled quickly, either before you leave, or at the picnic site, when people can choose their own combination of bread and filling. Most kitchen cupboards and refrigerators will reveal something suitable for sandwich fillings, and if you have time, you could even take the opportunity to create something really special in addition to the classic standbys such as eggs, cheese, and cold meat. You could also pick up freshly baked bread and rolls on the way to the picnic, especially as there are nearly always some shops open, wherever you are and whatever the day of the week.

Take salad ingredients cut into chunky pieces; carrots, cucumber, celery, and zucchini are ideal, and so are the small hearty crisp type of lettuce, as the tiny leaves are strong enough to use for scooping up dips. Salad dressings can easily be taken separately in screw-top containers for dunking or spooning into a salad sandwich. Unless you are eating quite near your home, it is better to add the dressing to a salad when you actually arrive and set up the picnic, as the dressing may make the salad soggy if left for too long.

Something sweet to finish off a picnic is always popular, but it needn't be an elaborate dessert; it can just as easily be fresh fruit, cakes, and cookies, although pies and tarts always go down well. Consider taking individual yogurts, ice creams, or even a frozen gâteau, if you have a freezer box to keep them in while the savory food is being eaten.

Something to drink is essential and having a freezer box will definitely be an advantage. Sparkling drinks may get too fizzed up if the trip is bumpy, so be very cautious when opening these, but wines, canned drinks, fruit juices, and so on all travel well. Take some bottled water as well, as the drinks always seem to run out!

FRENCH DRESSING

The amount of olive oil used may be varied to suit your taste. When made, store in a bottle or airtight container, and keep in a cool place for up to 10 days. Shake vigorously before each use.

4 tbsp olive oil
4 tbsp sunflower, corn, or
    vegetable oil
1 tbsp lemon juice (fresh or
    bottled)
salt and pepper
$1/2$ tsp dried mustard powder
$1/2$ tsp superfine sugar
1 garlic clove, crushed

1. Put all the ingredients either into a screw-top jar, and shake vigorously until completely emulsified; or place in a bowl, and whisk thoroughly until emulsified.
2. Taste and adjust the seasonings.

Variations:
Use a flavored vinegar such as tarragon; or add 1–2 tablespoons freshly chopped mixed herbs or one single herb; or add 2–3 tablespoons strained raspberries, blackberries, or blackcurrants for a fruit vinaigrette.

MAYONNAISE

Mayonnaise is not as difficult to make as it is often thought to be, but it is essential that all the ingredients are at room temperature before you start – chilled ingredients make curdling much more likely. The flavor can be varied widely by using a flavored vinegar instead of wine or cider vinegar, and many flavorings can be added for variations. When made, pack in a plastic, glass, or other container with a secure lid, and chill until required. It will keep in the refrigerator for about a week in prime condition. Use a fairly mild oil, but if you want to use olive oil, it is best to use only half olive and half a lighter flavored oil.

2 egg yolks
about 1 tbsp white wine
    vinegar or lemon juice
$1/2$ tsp made mustard
$1 1/4$ cups oil (vegetable,
    sunflower, or olive oil)
salt and pepper
good pinch of superfine sugar

1. Put the egg yolks into a bowl with 1 teaspoon of the vinegar or lemon juice and the mustard. Beat until thoroughly blended, using a balloon whisk or hand-held electric mixer.
2. Whisk in the oil a drop at a time, definitely no faster, until about a third of the oil has been added and the mixture begins to thicken.

PACKING AND TRANSPORTING THE FOOD

Packing and transporting a picnic has been made much easier thanks to the huge range of rigid plastic and other containers with securely fitting lids that is now available. Along with plastic wrap and foil, it is possible to transport almost anything, although some kinds of food will inevitably travel better than others. Lids and coverings are also important, for wherever you choose to picnic, a number of flies are almost certain to join you!

Foil is best for closely wrapping such things as meat, pastry items, and pâtés, but if the food is at all acidic, this may cause pitting to the foil, and a layer of plastic wrap or baking parchment should be used first, under the foil. If it is a food with a high fat content, such as cheese, you should use a suitable food wrap and not just regular plastic wrap for wrapping. Even rolls and sandwiches will arrive as if they have been freshly made when they are wrapped properly.

One or more good, sturdy insulated "cold" boxes or picnic baskets will, of course, help greatly with the transporting of the food. Obviously, begin by placing the heavier items at the bottom, but also try to put the desserts, fruit, and sweet food there, so it can be unpacked and used more or less in the order it is to be eaten. Always stand up anything than might seep if it tipped over, wedging it between other items. It may be an idea to carry chilled wine, beer and other drinks in a separate cold box, as often these are required first, and it will avoid turning the food upside-down in the haste to find the drinks! It also

means that the picnickers can enjoy a leisurely drink before the food is unpacked and laid out, which will insure that your picnic is a civilized affair.

Individual insulated "cold" bags or coolers, which can be used on a dinner table, are ideal for keeping wine or beer cool once opened. If you are picnicking by a river, take a net so the bottles can safely be dangled into the water for cooling.

Foods that do not have to be kept cool can be packed into shopping bags or boxes to stand upright in the back or trunk of the car. It is a good idea to place small cardboard boxes inside larger bags, in order to help everything to stay upright when the bag is picked up. Don't pack the chilled food until the last minute – and don't forget to add the ice blocks to insulated boxes before you finally close the lids!

INCLEMENT WEATHER

When the weather is likely to be less than warm and sunny, take full advantage of the wide range of vacuum and insulated thermos containers available. Many thermos containers have wide necks, so it is quite easy to take a simple stew or casserole in one and hot cooked rice in another; and, of course, always take plenty of hot soup, coffee, tea, and hot chocolate. Hot sausages can successfully be packed into thermos containers, but alternatively they can be securely wrapped in foil, along with baked potatoes, garlic bread, and rolls, and stacked in an insulated box, which is usually used for keeping things cold, but, like a vacuum flask, is just as good at keeping things hot. Certain types of the ice blocks used for these boxes can be heated in boiling water, and added to the box to keep the heat in. Obviously, this will not keep the food warm for hours on end, nor will the food taste its best if kept warm for too long, but the heat will last for several hours – we do this every year when taking a bunch of children on their ponies for a Christmas ride at the beach to be followed by soup, hot dogs, and burgers.

Another idea is to take a portable bottled gas stove for a kettle or saucepan of soup, but always be very careful where it is set up because if the wind increases or the portable gas stove falls over, it is a dangerous fire hazard. The safest way to set it up is to pile rocks around it, or bury it a few inches into the ground, and not to set it near bushes or trees, nor too near the car.

OTHER ESSENTIALS
Depending on the type of picnic you are having, you will need a blanket or two, or portable chairs, perhaps a portable table and tablecloth, along with paper napkins or a roll of paper towels. If the ground is a little damp, use a groundsheet under the blankets, or the plastic bags to be used later for collecting the garbage. Whether to use paper, plastic, or china plates is your own choice; food always tastes better off china, but, of course, paper is easier to dispose of, and plastic is lighter and safer to carry than china. Always remember to take a couple of large garbage bags for easy disposal of everything at the end of the picnic. Never leave garbage behind,

as it spoils the site for anyone else who uses it after you, and empty bottles, cans, plastic bags or plastic wrap can cause immense damage and pain to animals and huge vets' bills to their owners. Garbage bags are also good for carrying home the dirty plates and containers.

Don't take the best flatware unless you are dining out in style (and probably will then have someone to help clear up afterwards!), but make sure you have at least one really sharp or serrated knife, condiments, scissors (most useful), a corkscrew and a bottle opener, and a damp cloth carried in a plastic bag with a couple of clean dishcloths. It's not as if you are going to wash any dishes, but a clean cloth is always useful, particularly if there are small children around, who seem always to be covered in food, sand, or dirt!

If you are planning a stylish picnic on a summer's day, it can be nice to take a large parasol, if it can be stuck in the ground, or has its own base that can easily be transported. When packing the car, put the chairs, table, and blankets in last, so they can be removed first and set up before the food is unpacked.

If you think your guests might feel energetic after eating, take along a frisbee, bats and balls, or just a tennis ball for an impromptu game of catch. If you are making a day of it, it is often nice to have something to do rather than simply lie around contemplating the remains of the food! And finally, don't forget to take the insect bite cream, and a basic first-aid kit,because if you are well equipped for all eventualities, they will probably not be needed!

3. Add another teaspoonful of the vinegar or lemon juice and then continue to whisk in the oil, but now in a very thin trickle. It must be whisked briskly all the time. When it begins to really thicken, the oil can be added a little faster.
4. Season to taste with salt, pepper, and sugar, and add more vinegar or lemon juice if wished to give the desired flavor. If too thick, whisk in 1–2 tablespoons hot water. Store in an airtight container, in the refrigerator.

Variations:
Curried: Add 1–2 teaspoons curry powder and, if liked, 1–2 tablespoons finely chopped mango chutney.

Green: Add half bunch very finely chopped watercress with 2–3 finely chopped scallions, if liked.

Horseradish: Add 1–2 tablespoons creamed horseradish, or 2–3 teaspoons horseradish sauce to the mayonnaise or to taste.

Mustard: Add 2–3 tablespoons coarse grain mustard and a pinch of finely grated lemon rind.

Citrus: Add the finely grated rind of 1 orange or $1\frac{1}{2}$–2 lemons.

INDEX